First Edition
Public Information Officer

Michelle Charlesworth
Contract Writer

Michael D. Finney
Project Manager

Cynthia Brakhage
Editor

Validated by the International Fire Service Training Association
Published by Fire Protection Publications, Oklahoma State University

---

Cover photo courtesy of Oklahoma City (OK) Fire Department

RECYCLABLE

ISBN 0-87939-170-7
Library of Congress 99-67503

First Edition
First Printing, October 1999
Second Printing, July 2000

Order Number 36340

Printed in the United States of America

CONTENTS

Preface

This first edition of the *Public Information Officer* manual has been written to help fire department personnel understand and function in the role of PIO or department spokesperson. It conforms to the requirements of NFPA 1035, *The Professional Qualifications for Public Fire and Life Safety Educator*, 1999 edition.

Much time and effort go into the design, development, layout, and printing of any publication. This manual is no exception. Acknowledgement and special thanks are extended to the members of the IFSTA validation committee who contributed their time, wisdom, and knowledge to this manual.

IFSTA Validation Committee

Chair
Ed Kirtley
Guymon Fire Department
Guymon, Oklahoma

Committee Members

Jimmie Badgett
Dallas County Fire Marshal's Office
Dallas, Texas

Jon Hansen (Retired)
Oklahoma City Fire Department
Oklahoma City, Oklahoma

Penny Hulse
Pierce County Fire District #5
Gig Harbor, Washington

Jeffrey Johnson
Tualatin Valley Fire and Rescue
Aloha, Oregon

Bob Kahn
Phoenix Fire Department
Phoenix, Arizona

William Neville
Neville Associates
Penn Valley, California

Gratitude is also extended to the following members of the Fire Protection Publications staff whose contributions made the final publication of this manual possible:

Don Davis, Graphics Coordinator, Fire Protection Publications
Ann Moffat, Graphic Design Analyst
Desa Porter, Senior Graphic Designer
Ben Brock, Graphics Specialist
Mac Crank, Contract Artist

Foreword

In the Information Age, which we live in today, the media can either be your "best friend" or your "worst enemy" in a crisis situation. This publication is dedicated to helping other members of the fire service understand the media and learn how to develop good relations with the media. The key is striving to work with the media over the long term, instead of attempting to "manage" the media in any particular situation.

This book has been prepared for those who have little previous experience interacting with the media. In fact, we started out from that same point ourselves, so we know how you feel and have been down the road that lies before you now. Those who already serve as public information officers will also find the information presented in this book valuable because of the many suggestions gleaned from years of accumulated experience by the authors.

We have specially designed this manual to be user-friendly. We recommend that you read through the complete book. Then, keep it handy as a reference guide to help you respond to certain situations as they arise.

Good luck as you embark on your own set of exciting adventures with the media!

Sincerely

Jon A. Hansen

Introduction

The role of public information officer is very important to every department. While some agencies are able to assign the role on a permanent basis, others may assign the duty as needed. This manual was designed to assist any person who is asked to serve in the role of PIO or spokesperson at an emergency scene, as a representative of the department, or as the PIO as a routine assignment. It is intended for the individual who may be new to this role or the more seasoned PIO. Both will gain insightful information from the text. The manual is based upon NFPA 1035, *The Professional Qualifications for Public Fire and Life Safety Educator*, 1999 edition.

An Introduction to Public Information

An Introduction to Public Information

Information that at one time took hours or days to disseminate can now be sent nationally and internationally in a matter of seconds. Therefore, the media can provide late-breaking news as it happens and in great detail. In response to this advancement in technology, the fire department has developed the need for personnel who have the ability to meet the challenges of this changing environment and can work with the media with confidence and poise.

The public information function is vital to maintaining and improving the image of the fire department; therefore, the public information officer (PIO) is extremely important to the organization. The PIO serves as the department's spokesperson and is responsible for disseminating information to the media at disasters and emergency incidents. The PIO provides education to the public, promotes public safety, and talks about services that the department provides. As a PIO, your ultimate goal is to enhance the public perception of the department. Because the public's perception of the fire department is greatly formed through the media, the PIO needs to have the ability to effectively communicate with the media — which will result in a good working relationship with the media.

However, enhancing your organizational reputation should not be confused with "image engineering." No effort should ever be made to develop an image that is not reflective of your organizational responsibilities. The fire service provides a broad range of services that are often unknown to the public. The public may also be unaware of the value that the fire department adds to the community. Communicating that value and professionalism as well as informing the community about your department's activities will yield an enhanced reputation.

Figure 1.1 *Courtesy of Oklahoma City (Oklahoma) Fire Department.*

COMMUNICATIONS AND THE MEDIA

Communication is the ongoing process that individuals use to complete the exchange of information and attitudes. For the purposes of this book, it can be defined further as *the exchange of ideas and information that conveys an intended meaning in a form that is understood.* It is the process by which individuals interact to impart knowledge and to influence each other.[1] The ideas or information that people exchange is often called the *message.* The channel or system that a person uses to communicate the message is called the *medium* (plural *media*). (**NOTE:** Today, the term *media* is used commonly as a collective noun referring to "the mass media.")

Mass media are publications, broadcasts, and visuals that are designed to reach large numbers of individuals, and they usually carry advertising. Using the mass media to communicate a message is not as simple as it appears. Communication is much more than sharing an idea with another person. Effective communication does not take place unless the receiver of the message provides the sender with appropriate *feedback* (a response that demonstrates understanding). The public information officer must not only know what information to provide to the media but also be able to communicate effectively so that this information is received, understood, and acted upon.

UNDERSTANDING WHAT MAKES NEWS

While most local fire service stories lack the inherent hard news value of national events, there is generally ample community interest in the information to warrant sharing it. Therefore, many of these soft news stories are broadcast or printed locally. Local media and the community at large are usually interested in meetings, rallies, seminars, open houses, and educational activities, such as public education programs.

Public statements on local affairs, awards given and received, fund drives, calls for membership, promotions, new equipment acquisitions, and the appointment or resignation of local officials also generate considerable community interest. The goal is to help the media understand how your story meets their needs for news.

Two types of information will be sought by the media — information pertaining to your department and emergency scene information. As the PIO, you may be asked to serve in one or both roles as the department spokesperson and the incident PIO.

The Department Spokesperson

In order to be an effective spokesperson, you must understand the organizational structure and the administrative goals and policies of your department. You must also know how to access top administrators of the emergency organization so that your information is as correct as possible. Never get your information secondhand — always go to the source. This allows you to answer questions in accordance to departmental policy and jurisdictional law. Another way to be informed is to make every effort to be directly involved in department policy level meetings.

The Incident PIO

At an emergency scene, the incident commander (IC) is responsible for the dissemination of information unless this duty is delegated to the PIO. First and foremost, it is your responsibility to understand the technical terms used by fire department personnel.

Members of the media are the eyes and ears of the public and the conduits of information to the public.

Members of the media are your allies — not your enemies.

Members of the media are customers with needs to be met.

This enables you to accurately convey to the media what is happening on the scene. In short, it is your responsibility to gather the information from the IC and other sources, translate it into understandable messages for the public, and then relay it to reporters.

SUMMARY

Public information is an integral part of the organization and the incident management system. To develop a strong program within your organization, you need a clear understanding of the roles of the department spokesperson and the PIO. You must also understand how to effectively communicate with the media and the public. Effective public information is crucial to the success of any department or organization.

> ### The Public Information Officer Creed
>
> I will conduct myself with honesty and integrity.
>
> What I communicate has an impact, either good or bad, on the organization.
>
> I have a duty to consider the rights of those I serve, including my own personnel.
>
> I have a responsibility to ensure the safety of the media at the emergency scene.
>
> I have the responsibility to enhance public perception of the department.
>
> I need to push information to the media — and not force the media to pull it from me.

Chapter One Notes

1. James F. Evans, "Education Campaign Planning," course reference, University of Illinois, 1985, p. 3-2.

Chapter 2

The Public Information Officer

In Chapter 1, we reviewed the PIO's responsibility to serve as the department's liaison with the media. This role allows you to enhance the public's perception of the department, to inform the public of the department's emergency operations, and to educate the public on fire and life safety topics. To effectively fulfill these responsibilities, the PIO must present his or her very best at all times. Remember, as PIO, you may be asked to fill the role of department spokesperson or incident PIO at any given time.

DESIRABLE CHARACTERISTICS OF THE PIO

The following characteristics are critical for achieving success as a PIO (Figure 2.1):

- *Be honest*. The PIO must be honest. This characteristic is absolutely crucial to establishing and maintaining credibility with the media, with the public, and with fire personnel. There is never a situation that warrants being dishonest. A simple lie could easily destroy the trust that you have developed with the media — a trust that will be very difficult to restore.

- *Be accurate.* The media and the public count on you to make sure that the information you provide is accurate. Facts and figures about emergency incidents, such as fire loss, number of personnel at the scene, and response times, must be factual. Remember that the information you provide is not only a matter of public record, it may also be used during litigation. The PIO must be willing to search out accurate facts and present them in a manner which is easily understood by the public and the media.

Organized

Honest

Creates a Professional Image

Keeps Commitments

Expertise in Public Information

Accurate with Information

Effective Communicator

Accessible to Media

Accessible to Internal Customer

The PIO

Figure 2.1 Desirable characteristics of a public information officer.

- *Create a professional image*. The PIO is the personification of the values of the department. Because of this, you must dress in a manner that portrays the department in a positive way. Poor dress and/or grooming leads the public and the media to believe that this is the norm for your department. Your goal should be to ensure that you meet the professional expectations of the department and that they meet the cultural and social norms of the community. A final thought about professional appearance is that you must remember that you are always "on-duty" as the PIO. You must not only act the part, but you must also be careful in social situations. The manners you project must portray what is considered to be socially acceptable. This is not always easy because what is socially acceptable is defined differently by nearly everyone. But, there is certainly an acceptable norm in your community which you must observe.

- *Be accessible.* The PIO must always be accessible to the media and to other members of the department. You are in the information and communication business. To be successful, people who have the information must be able to reach you. In addition, the people who want the information must also be able to get the information when they need it.

  You must also be easily accessible at the emergency scene to both the media and the incident commander. Your position requires you to act as a staff support officer for the incident commander and to give the media the information they need. This requires being accessible to both parties during the incident. Accessibility is further discussed in Chapters 4 and 9. If you will be unavailable for a length of time, the responsibilities of this vital position must then be transferred to a designated person who can fulfill those duties in your absence.

- *Follow up on commitments.* One of the characteristics of a PIO most appreciated by the media is the PIO's ability to follow up on commitments. Timely follow-up on requests for information is one of the best ways to gain trust and respect. In fact, the best follow-up is to provide the information before it is needed or requested. This approach is called "pushing" information. If members of the media must contact you after an incident to get information, they are placed in a position of "pulling" the information from you, and this is not a good situation. The successful PIO anticipates the media's needs and immediately follows up after an incident, providing the information as it is available.

  In addition, when arranging to provide a specific piece of information, such as an interview or something similar, be willing to meet that commitment. Broken commitments result in broken trust. When you lose the trust of the media, you lose your ability to be effective as a PIO.

- *Communicate effectively.* In order for the media and the community to get the information they want and need, the PIO must be able to effectively communicate. Part of this is the ability to communicate verbally in a manner that is easily understood. You must also be able to properly compose news releases and media advisories. Finally, the information must be communicated in a format that is usable. This may require that you meet with your local media to find out the format it desires or attend media or communication training programs. The bottom line is that you are responsible for getting the information to the media in a format that is usable and in a style that can be easily understood by the public.

- *Be organized*. You must make every effort to be organized. This helps when you need to answer questions or to provide follow-up information. You should maintain a current list of media contacts. You should also have ready access to background information on the department and information on pertinent statistics, such as fire loss and the number of annual fire incidents. This type of information is frequently requested by the media, and it can be used to enhance stories. You must also be aware of local topics and current events so that you understand how the fire department's programs and services affect local issues.

- *Develop expertise*. You must have certain knowledge and experience in order to succeed in the role of the PIO. It is very helpful to have a knowledge of operations, which includes the following:

— Services provided by the organization

— Basics of emergency operations that are performed by the department

— Organization of the fire department

— Incident management system used by your department

— Department personnel who can help you with questions you cannot answer

It is also essential that you have expertise in the area of public information. This includes understanding how your local media functions, the needs of the media, the proper methods for disseminating information to the media, and effective methods for conducting media interviews. If you do not have these skills, it is your responsibility to seek out training opportunities and experiences which will help develop these skills.

CATEGORIES OF RESPONSIBILITY FOR THE PUBLIC INFORMATION OFFICER

The PIO generally concentrates his or her efforts in three categories: public information, public relations, and public education. A working knowledge of each is critical to the success of the PIO, as each category is dependent upon the other. Each category is discussed and defined below.

Public Information

Public information is the dissemination of information about emergency incidents and other significant department issues. This information includes fire loss, fire injuries, EMS operations, construction of new facilities, fiscal issues, etc. Public information may also include policy issues, such as staffing at fire stations and new safety rules.

Public Relations

Public relations is the development of a positive public perception about the department and its operations and services. While it is true that public information may result in the enhancement of public perception, this is not its focus. Its focus is to disseminate information about programs, services, and achievements of the department. For example, a department implements a new program that provides free smoke detectors to low-income families. The PIO is tasked with ensuring that the community is aware of the program and its benefits.

Public Education

The goal of the public education function is to change behaviors, which leads to a reduction in preventable fires and injuries. The PIO is in a unique position to be able to accomplish this goal. When a fire occurs, the media is very interested in stories that create a teachable moment for public education, and the story should include ways in which the fire could be prevented. The story may also emphasize how proper fire and life safety procedures prevented a fire or injuries. For example, a PIO responds to a residential fire that was caused by food left unattended on the stove. However, the family had a working smoke detector that went off and gave the family time to get out of the house. The PIO should emphasize how the fire could have been prevented and the fact that a working smoke detector gave the family time to get out of the house.

The PIO must emphasize fire and life safety issues whenever the opportunity arises. The PIO must seek every opportunity to teach life safety skills and attitudes when the public is listening. Whenever possible, the PIO should coordinate these efforts with the department's public fire and life safety educator.

THE PIO AND THE INTERNAL CUSTOMER

One of the forgotten aspects of being an effective PIO is the need to establish and maintain a positive relationship with the members of the organization and the other organizations with whom you work. Your best sources of information about what is happening in the department are the men and women inside the department. It is these people who are implementing new programs and providing emergency services and who are aware of unusual stories and events that are newsworthy. It is your job to tell the story about the men and women of the department and what they do to serve the community. If you do this consistently, they will provide you with all the information that you will ever need.

If you fail to take care of the internal customer, your best source of information will evaporate. And be aware that this can happen very easily. As the PIO, you will constantly be in front of the public: on television, on the radio, and quoted in the paper. It is easy for you to become the center of attention rather than those who are doing the job. At every opportunity you must be telling the story of the men and women who are out there doing the job of the department. Do not become the focus of the story at the expense of your relationship with the other personnel in the department. The best rule to follow is to give credit where credit is due.

MANAGING THE DEPARTMENT IMAGE

Every fire department has an image in its community. One of your goals should be to improve that image through effective public information activities. The media will be your conduit to communicating important department information to the public. Information reported in the proper manner will enhance the reputation and credibility of the department.

The goal of enhancing the department image also involves being open with the public. There may be times that you may have to provide information that is not favorable to the department. This must always be done in cooperation with the leaders of the department and must also be done with integrity on your part. Just as you must always be honest with the media, you must also be honest with the public. It is generally in the best interest of the department to admit its mistakes, take accountability for its actions, and then do the best to make sure that it does not happen again. It will be your job to convey those messages to the public in a forthright manner that will not destroy the credibility and trust you have established.

SUMMARY

As the PIO, you have the chance to make a very positive difference in the way the public views the department. To accomplish this, you must act with integrity, serve both internal and external customers, and develop the expertise necessary to effectively communicate your organizational achievements.

Chapter 3
Ethics, Legal Issues, and Policies

One of the PIO's most important tools is his or her ability to develop and maintain a relationship with the media and the public that is built on trust. Establishing this trust is necessary to develop credibility, which is essential if the PIO is to be successful in his or her job. While there are many traits that affect the building of trust, the PIO acting ethically and according to the law are two of the most important. This chapter addresses the ethical, legal, and policy issues that direct the actions of the PIO.

ETHICS

Ethics is defined as principles of good conduct. In the case of the PIO, it means acting in an manner that is based on honesty and integrity. Acting ethically is never simply a part-time necessity. Acting ethically is an every-time, all-the-time requirement of any PIO.

The following are some of the ethical behaviors that apply to the PIO.

- *Always tell the truth.* This must be the credo for the PIO. Deceiving the media, and subsequently the public, is never acceptable. If there is an issue which cannot be discussed at that time, tell the media. If you don't know the answer, say "I don't know" and then work to find the answer. Remember that if you deceive the media, you will never again be trusted.

- *Protect the interests and welfare of the public.* The events surrounding many incidents can be very painful or embarrassing to those involved. While you must certainly disclose all information as required by law, you must also do what you can to ensure that the feelings and needs of those involved in the incident are also considered and when appropriate protected from public disclosure.

- *Protect the interests and welfare of department personnel.*

- *Treat all members of the media fairly.* You may develop close working relationships with specific members of the media and be tempted to provide them the "special" stories. However, you must treat all members of the media fairly regardless of your relationship with them.

- *Hold the media accountable for fair and accurate reporting.* You also have an ethical responsibility on behalf of your department to ensure that the media is accurately and fairly reporting stories about the department and its personnel.

- *Release information that pertains only to the fire department.* The PIO should only provide information to the media that pertains to the activities of his or her department unless specifically authorized to do so by other agencies. This can be an issue at multi-jurisdictional operations and is addressed in Chapter 10.

LEGAL ISSUES

Your actions as a PIO are also governed by applicable local, state/provincial, and federal laws. In the United States, most of the laws pertaining to public information are based on the First Amendment to the U.S. Constitution, also known as Freedom of the Press. Freedom of the Press guarantees the legal right to the media to gather and disseminate information to the public on the actions and activities of government. Supreme Court decisions have even expanded the media's rights under the constitution to include the obligation to report on the activities of government.

It is essential that every PIO seek guidance from the department's attorney regarding laws relating to public information in his or her community. This step must be taken before implementing the public information function in the department or assigning a person to the duties of PIO. This prevents the PIO from violating the law and possibly incurring civil and criminal penalties.

Figure 3.1 *Courtesy of Oklahoma City (Oklahoma) Fire Department.*

Legal principles which affect the PIO's activities are listed below. Again, you must confer with your department's legal counsel to clarify how each principle applies in your community.

- *Open records.* Most states and provinces have laws which require that government records be open for public review. This includes writings, reports, correspondence, etc., used in the day-to-day course of business. This means that the PIO may have to release department records and reports to the media. However, there are some records which are protected. These include records and reports used in current criminal investigations, some types of personnel information, and medical information on employees.

- *Release of information.* Some states have established time limits on the release of information to the public and the media. These time limits require government agencies to release requested information within a specific time following a request.

- *Open view.* This is one of the most misunderstood laws regarding public information. The open view principle allows the media to video, photograph, or record anything that is in the open view of the public. In other words, if the public at an incident can observe the fire department's operations, the media may capture those scenes and sounds and use them in news stories. The PIO's first instinct may be to block the media from taking pictures at some scenes. However, if the scene is in open view of the public, the media has the right to take the pictures.

- *Personal medical records.* Generally, the law recognizes most of the information contained in EMS incident reports to be part of the patient's personal medical report, especially information about a person's history of infectious disease. This information is protected by the law and can only be released to the media with the patient's permission. When addressing EMS incidents, the PIO must provide only general information about the types of injuries and the action taken by the department.

- *Criminal investigations.* Any incident information that is part of an ongoing criminal investigation, such as an arson investigation, is protected from release. It is very important that the PIO work closely with investigators, detectives, and prosecutors to ensure that only approved facts and information are released to the media regarding such incidents. The premature release of information may compromise the investigation and legal action against the suspected criminals. Also, many states do not allow the release of the names of minors involved in crimes, such as arson, even after adjudication by the courts.

- *Access to private property.* When a fire department responds to a fire or rescue, the law provides the department with the authority to enter the property and mitigate the situation. However, the law does not grant the department the authority to allow the media to enter the property and take video or photographs. It is the responsibility of the PIO to protect the owner's right to privacy during and after emergency operations. If there is something that would enhance a story, especially a fire or life safety teachable moment, the PIO should seek permission from the owner to allow the media onto the property to get the desired video or photographs.

- *Personnel records.* The personnel records maintained by local government are generally public records. However, some parts of an employee's personnel file, such as medical information, the nature of disciplinary actions, and promotional/hiring test scores, may be protected. Again, you must confer with the department attorney to identify which parts of the personnel record are protected by the law.

- *Disclosures of the names of fatalities.* Generally, the law does not protect the release of the names of people, including minors, who die or are injured in fires or crashes. The exception is when there is a criminal investigation of the incident, for example, when foul play may be suspected. This legal principle requires the PIO to carefully consider each situation and ensure that the needs of the victim's family are considered while also disseminating the information to the media in a timely manner. Many departments do have policies requiring notification of next of kin before the names are released to the media.

DEPARTMENT POLICIES

Every department should adopt specific policies which guide the public information function. These policies should identify the following:

- Type of information that can be routinely released by the PIO or other department personnel to the media

- Personnel who are authorized to act as an official department spokesperson on administrative and policy issues

- Steps for processing media and public requests for department records, reports, etc.

- Specific information that cannot be released to the media without approval from the department administration and/or legal counsel

- Process for notifying next of kin when an incident involves a fatality or serious injury

- Role and responsibilities and authority of the PIO — a job description

- Responsibilities and authority of the "information" position in the incident management system used by the department

- Process for addressing any problems or issues with the media

A good resource to use when developing department policies are the policies currently being used by other departments. Once the policies have been drafted, they should be reviewed by the department's legal counsel. It may also be beneficial to have a member of the media review the draft policies to ensure that the rights and needs of the media are protected. This media input may prevent problems in the future, and it helps build a relationship of trust with the media. The final step in adoption of the policies is for the department head to approve the policies and then communicate them to all department personnel who may be involved in the release of information.

SUMMARY

The PIO's actions are guided by laws, department policies, and ethical principles. The laws and policies are designed to protect the rights of the media, the public, and the department. It is the responsibility of the PIO to understand the laws and policies and then to apply them in an ethical manner in every situation.

Chapter 4 The Media

Mention the word media, and a number of connotations come to mind. Fire departments have seen beneficial results as well as devastating consequences from the local media's coverage of emergency scene operations. However the department may view the media, it is nonetheless a strong and influential part of society. How the department relates to the media and uses it as a tool can greatly enhance the department's relationship with the community as a whole.

In many ways, the members of the media function much like the personnel of a fire department. The media — as well as fire department personnel — must follow their organizations' chain of command. As well, each media organization has divisions and specialties, such as sports, national news, local news, and weather, that work together to benefit the organization. Although the fire department is one organization, each person brings a specialized skill that benefits the organization as a whole. Each fire department member is an integral part of the team — media personnel function in the same manner. Each reporter may have a different specialty or focus, such as sports or national news, but the contribution benefits the entire organization.

Media personnel view themselves as objective and impartial. They believe their role to be guardians of the public interest. Reporters, as well as fire department members, have a niche within the community because of the services they provide. Therefore, the community holds members of the fire department and the media accountable for their actions. As the public information officer, the best means for you to quickly and effectively reach and inform the public is through the media. To successfully promote the fire department's goals and aims, you must make every effort to create and maintain positive relationships with media personnel. This begins by having a better understanding of the media organizations and how they do their job. The media does not like to be told what to say or how to say it; in other words, do not try to manage news.

CHARACTERISTICS OF MEDIA ORGANIZATIONS

The resources available for transferring information from one source to another have created an incredible variety in which to gather and transmit news to the public. Modern technology has opened doors unimaginable to prior generations. This will expand even more as technology continues to grow and develop. The forms of media the PIO should be familiar with include print, radio, television, and computers. The PIO should also be familiar with those available within the community and how to best use these resources for the department.

Print

Print media gives the reader detailed information, fits into the reader's time constraints, and can be saved for future reference.

Daily newspapers cover a wide range of topics delivered to an even wider range of readers. Typically, daily newspapers go into great depth on stories to include photos and other pertinent information. They typically will have a deadline of 8 p.m. to 10 p.m. for morning editions but can hold deadlines until later if late-breaking news warrants it.

Weekly newspapers typically address a specific audience such as a local community, an ethnic group, or a group with a shared interest. These newspapers also may include stories with in-depth information and facts but would focus the story toward a specific audience. These stories require packaged facts and statistics . Weekly newspapers usually have a 24-48 hour deadline before printing.

There are two types of stories that apply to print media — stories and briefs. A *story* is a very detailed-oriented article that may address a broad range of issues. It may include photographs, especially action shots, and quotes may be somewhat lengthy. A *brief* is an abbreviated story on local events that gives only the basic facts of the event or issue. Quotes may not be verbatim, and it may not include photographs.

Radio

Another form of media is the radio. For obvious reasons, radio brings with it unique elements that the print media does not address. The ability to hear sound and bring the news immediately to listeners into a variety of places, such as the

home, vehicle, or office, gives this form of media a different twist. When working with radio personnel, you should remember the following:

- Radio programming is fast-paced, sound-bite oriented, and broadcast instantly.

- The audience includes a variety of listeners in various locations; therefore, it is easy to target a specific group.

- Radio has hourly deadlines because it is always live.

- Programming may be interactive, such as talk shows, where you receive on-air questions from listeners.

- Radio reaches large numbers of people quickly.

Television

Television is the ideal medium for communications. Television has become the heart and soul of the community and of the home. Television brings to the viewer many characteristics such as sight, sound, motion, and accessibility. With television, the viewer can watch the news as well as hear the report. This allows for a visual impact of the events. Television brings with it the following characteristics:

- It is headline-oriented (much like the prior two forms of media). The reporter needs to get the viewer's attention without sensationalizing.

- It can give segments in 60 seconds or less.

- It is fast-paced, action-oriented, and highly competitive.

- It may have aerial shots or provide more access for the viewer.

- The deadline for television is usually two hours before a broadcast.

- Programming themes will differ for the morning, noon, and night news.

The advent of various cable news networks has also changed the way news is presented. Some cable networks present news 24 hours a day with stories updated at regular intervals throughout the day. This creates different deadlines for different stations depending on their organizational policies. Also, many local communities have developed their own local public access channels. This creates even greater opportunities for the department to have presence within the community.

Electronic
Electronic media has brought the ability to quickly release news and events. Electronic media includes computers

COMMON MEDIA TERMINOLOGY

Assignment editor: The person at either radio, newspaper, or television news organizations that stays abreast of what is happening and assigns personnel to go out to cover stories.

Background video or B-roll: Also called "cover." Video that covers and matches the narration portion of the story. B-roll also can cover up a sound bite to better illustrate what the interviewee is saying.

Beat: A specific subject area assigned to a reporter.

City desk/assignment desk: Synonymous with the assignment editor.

Live shot: A live broadcast from a remote location via a microwave or satellite television truck.

Natural sound: The sound recorded on location. Usually gathered by the microphone mounted on the front of the camera. This is the sound that is associated with background video, B-roll, or cover.

Negatives or pics: Negatives are the original photographic images from which multiple prints can be made. Pics usually refer to prints.

Pool shot: A situation where the various news agencies agree to share a shot, video, or photographic opportunity that is accessible by only one photographer or reporter. Example: a courtroom trial where only one camera is allowed inside.

Sound bite: A portion of an interview, usually much shorter than the entire answer given by the interviewee.

Two shot: A shot, usually over the shoulder of the reporter, to be used as a cutaway during editing.

Voice-over: Narration audio that is played over video.

White balance: A setting on a video camera that tells it what shade of white is available in a given shot. There is a large difference between the color of white in indoor lighting versus outdoor lighting.

(especially with the advent of the Internet and video usage with computers), satellites, talk back TV programs, and distance learning. Electronic technology has opened a new and incredible arena for media. Now information can be delivered at an incredible rate of speed. Viewers can watch as events unfold in the comfort of their homes. This brings greater challenges for the department PIO. He or she will need to have a greater understanding of the medium and how it can impact his or her department.

Many fire departments have taken advantage of the Internet to begin posting their own web pages. Information can now be transmitted globally as well as locally with equal amount of quickness. While news can be released in fast-breaking segments, there can still be a great deal of detailed-oriented information. The Internet has opened many doors for communication. This form of media is quickly evolving and is always changing. This brings new challenges to the media in that it must provide the same amount of high quality information but with much shorter deadlines.

The electronic form of media has also changed the way departments work. Reports are now written on computer, e-mail can be transmitted throughout a department, and larger amounts of information can be stored in less space. For the public information officer, this allows for the ability to retrieve and send out information at a much greater pace.

BEYOND THE LOCAL MEDIA

There are times when the PIO may need to deal with media personnel from outside the local community. This may include media from other communities, national media personnel, and freelance personnel. When working with media from outside the local community, the PIO must make an effort to be fair and understanding and present a positive image of the community and the department. Often, the PIO most likely will be dealing with

the local affiliate of the national media, but he or she needs to be aware of the possibility that this will not always be the case.

Another point to keep in mind is that when the national media is involved, it has the potential to become a more time-consuming production because of an overwhelming number of people involved. The PIO should still use strong organizational skills and people skills to present a positive image of the community and department in which he or she serves.

Figure 4.1 *Courtesy of Michael Wieder.*

SUMMARY

The media provides a service to the community much like the fire department. Their end goals are very similar æ how to better serve the general public. The media can also be an excellent resource for the department to use. The PIO should create means to work in harmony rather than opposition with the media. The two organizations can provide a beneficial service to the community, but only if they work together.

Chapter 5

Developing Positive Relationships with the Media

In Chapter 2 we discussed the characteristics of the public information officer and established what the role of the PIO should encompass. However, the PIO will be ineffective unless positive relationships are established with the media. These relationships should begin as soon as a person assumes the role of the PIO. The methods used to accomplish this will vary from department to department. The PIO should research the techniques that other departments in their area have used to establish relationships with the media. Often, this research reveals what has and has not been effective. This may

Figure 5.1 *Courtesy of Phoenix (Arizona) Fire Department.*

help to alleviate making similar mistakes. Establishing positive relationships will enhance the following:

- Your effectiveness in getting the information to the public

- Your ability to communicate the department's side of a controversial issue

- The perception of your department

- Your credibility with the media

- Your access to the media

- Your ability to perform routine communications

HOW TO DEVELOP POSITIVE RELATIONSHIPS WITH THE MEDIA

Understanding how to develop positive relationships with the media is equally as important as understanding why we establish these relationships. The methods used may vary from department to department and should be carefully researched for effectiveness before trying this within your department. The following will help develop positive relationships with the media:

- Treat the media as customers.

- Develop and distribute a media guide.

- Create one-on-one relationships with members of the media.

- Understand the media's needs.

- Be proactive.

Treat the Media as a Customer

The first role of customer service is to exceed the expectations of the customer. Responding quickly to media inquiries with accurate, complete, and truthful information is the foundation for building a positive relationship. You must strive to help your customers overcome their obstacles, meet their deadlines, and see the complete story. Avoid sending media customers out of your "information store." They will go shopping for information elsewhere, which can only have negative results for you. Do not allow your daily frustrations to interfere with your relationship with your customers.

Develop and Distribute a Media Guide

An excellent step toward establishing positive relationships with the media is to help them understand the design and function of your department. This can be done a number of ways. For example, the **Oklahoma City (OK) Fire Department Media Guide** contains the following:

- The fire department's organizational chart, names, positions, radio numbers, and contact numbers.

- Definitions and explanations of fire department responsibilities.

- Information on the fire dispatch center and what the media should and should not expect from dispatch. It is also includes radio frequencies.

- A full explanation about identifying personnel at a scene, how an incident is rated, and what the media should and should not do at the scene.

- Explanations and definitions for the breakdown within its organization.

(Taken from the News Media Guide to the Oklahoma City Fire Department, Spirit 9 KWTV, prepared by Jon Hansen.)

Create One-on-One Relationships with the Media

As the department's PIO, it is important to establish relationships with the media and continue to strengthen these relationships. There are a number of benefits to doing this. First, one-on-one relationships can be used to strengthen the integrity of the department in which you work and can enhance your credibility as a PIO. Second, this allows for the increased consolidation of the needs of the media and the needs of the department. Third, it allows for recognition of behind-the-scene players. These include fire department personnel, other organizations' personnel, and anyone else involved in an incident. These players are important because they enable you to do your job. Finally, having a relationship that allows for candid discussions between you and the media will allow you to provide the background for decisions. An informed media is better able to provide objective reporting about your department's actions.

Understanding the Media

An important means to building relationships with the media is by first understanding its business and the needs it has (see Chapter 4). Having a working knowledge of what it does will also enhance your ability to meet its needs. It is important to remember that the media is not the enemy — it is simply meeting a need within the community, just as you are. Developing an understanding of what it does and training personnel within the department to understand the media will be an asset. Members of the media see themselves as the eyes and ears of the community. Be open, honest, and candid about issues preferably in advance of when the issue becomes topical.

Be Proactive

Take the initiative to build positive relationships with members of the media by using the following guidelines:

- Do not wait for the media to come looking for you to get the story.

- Give them opportunities to look good.

- Give advance notification of stories and upcoming events.

- Compliment them publicly when they do a good job of covering departmental events and scenes.

- Keep your commitments when you notify the media of news releases.

- Be accurate and honest in the information that you release and follow up in a timely manner.

Being proactive on your part requires some extra work, but it will greatly benefit the relationships established with the media.

CONFLICT RESOLUTION

Even with the greatest relationships, times of conflict will arise. During these times, do not allow this to damage your relationship with the media. Begin by resolving the conflicts off camera. The public arena is not the area to resolve differences.

COMPARISON OF THE HANDLING OF THE BEIRUT BOMBING AND THE WATERGATE SCANDAL

The comparison of President Nixon's cover-up of Watergate and President Reagan's handling of the Beirut bombing shows the positive results that President Reagan received from being honest and forthright. During the Watergate scandal, President Nixon made the decision to conceal or withhold information. Instead of accepting responsibility, he placed the blame on others.

In 1983, a marine headquarters was bombed by terrorists, and 190 people were killed. The marines were in Beirut because of the decision of President Reagan and Congress. Instead of placing blame on the terrorists or on Congress, President Reagan took full responsibility for what happened on the day that it happened. He did not wait for the incident to grow. What could have become a major incident during President Reagan's term is now nearly forgotten by those not affected by this tragedy. This incident obviously involved much more than Watergate and its cover-up because lives were lost. However, President Reagan did not face negative publicity because of the way he handled the event.

By taking responsibility and admitting mistakes immediately, you will hopefully be able to avoid a negative outcome.

An excellent way to begin is to objectively look at the situation from the media's standpoint. By doing so, you may be able to gain a better understanding of its views as they pertain to the situation. You should also attempt to find a common ground on which the media can understand your point of view as the PIO and that of your department as well. Sometimes achieving this understanding may require the help of a third party. Once this has been accomplished together, try to come to a compromise in which the interests of both parties have been met. At all cost, remain professional and try not to interpret conflict as the final battlefield.

DEVELOP A MEANS TO MUTUAL COOPERATION

As the PIO, take advantage of opportunities for cooperation on community issues and affairs. This may include community events that promote departmental goals, disasters in which the community "pulled together" to overcome, or mutual human interest stories. The feature here is to show a positive working relationship with those who report the information to the general public. A suggestion is to work with the editor on news releases. When reviewing publications, ask yourself these three questions:

- Was the story in the best interest of the fire department?

- Was the story in the best interest of the media outlet?

- Was the story in the best interest of the community?

It may be beneficial to join the local press club. This will give you the firsthand opportunity to understand the job of the media and its needs.

MEDIA SAFETY

Many departments are developing programs to help the media understand the need for safety on the scene. These are simply orientation programs that teach the media the department's needs for safety on the fireground and why it is important to meet these needs. Helping the media understand this before the incident will facilitate your job on the fireground.

Many departments are now adopting programs similar to that of the Phoenix Fire Department Certified Journalist Academy, even if it is on a more limited basis. It has helped to develop a better understanding and working relationship between emergency service providers and the media.

PHOENIX FIRE DEPARTMENT CERTIFIED JOURNALIST ACADEMY

The city of Phoenix understood how important the media was to its success in reaching the community. In turn, the fire department wanted the media to understand its various roles. Therefore, the Phoenix Fire Department's public information office started a 40-hour, 5-day certified fire journalist academy.

Journalists participating in the academy learn about the fireground, fire, rescue procedures, vehicle driving, and stress management. (Participating members of the media are loaned protective gear to use during this training.) Upon completion of the course, they are given certification certificates. This certification allows journalists to have closer access to an incident. This, in turn, will give the journalists a safer opportunity to get the story they need.

Not only do the media personnel who finish receive the benefits of getting better stories, they better understand the duties and roles involved with fire department personnel. The fire department also benefits. It is able to build positive relationships with these individuals. Both sides give and receive information and knowledge. This training is not intended to exclude any member of the media from access of information, but is meant to provide a better understanding of the department and its function.

(Taken from the Certified Fire Journalist Academy of the Phoenix Fire Department. For more information, contact the Public Information Office of the Phoenix Fire Department at (602) 534-0953.)

SUMMARY

As the PIO, positive working relationships are imperative for your success. Establishing and maintaining these relationships will be an ongoing part of your job.

Chapter 6
Gathering Information

Information is important to the success of any department. Therefore, the public information officer's ability to collect, manage, and disseminate information effectively will help determine the department's image. As the PIO, you must network within the organization and outside your department to provide informative and comprehensive information to the media and the general public. This requires you to be both proactive and reactive in your development of departmental data.

INTERNAL GATHERING OF DATA

Information management must begin within the department. It is not only important to be able to collect data, but you should also be able to interpret the data as well. Begin by monitoring statistical and historical data within the department.

It is important to have a thorough background of the type of calls the department typically runs, how often these calls are made, and a brief history on the calls. This provides the foundation information for reference and research. State and

PUBLIC INFORMATION NOTESHEET

1. Day/Night
2. Date
3. Times
4. Responded to Situation
5. Dept./Mutual Aid
6. Units/Apparatus
7. Agencies
8. Personnel
9. Reason Dispatched
10. Structure Size
11. Occupancy
12. Function
13. Owner's Name/Address
14. Occupant's Name/Address
15. How Reported
16. Situation
17. What Happened
18. Evacuation
19. Rescues
20. Health Hazards
21. Hazards
22. Injuries/Fatalities
23. Where Taken
24. Accomplishments
25. Fire Damage
26. Damage Estimates
27. Cause
28. Smoke Detectors
29. Contacts
30. Follow-Up
31. PE Message

Figure 6.1 Having preprinted note sheets for use on the scene helps to facilitate much of the PIO's work. A full-size copy of this document can be found on the disk included with the book.

national standards are excellent tools to use for this. By doing so, you may begin to see trends and patterns as well as comparisons of your department to others across the country.

You should keep informed of current trends within the field, such as in arson, fire prevention, and life safety, and be able to relay this information to your internal and external information customers. This information can be drawn from the data that you have maintained from statistical reports. As you review this material, look for patterns that may be forming. As with other information, compare this to state and national trends and patterns.

The PIO must develop relationships within the department and maintain this network of resources. If the PIO position is new to the department, this is even more crucial. PIOs may find that others within the organization may not initially accept this position and may even find it intrusive. To overcome these obstacles, you must constantly keep the PIO function visible to the internal organization and create a strong infrastructure of communication. This includes keeping informed of current investigations and current incidents. As individuals become more aware of the position and the positive impact it has on the department, acceptance will generally follow.

The PIO may sometimes find that he or she does not always have the luxury of time to accumulate information for the media. The PIO should attempt to gather as much information as possible before arrival on the scene by monitoring incident communications. It may also be helpful to contact the dispatch center for additional information.

Once on the scene, gather information from the field personnel such as the incident commander, operations chief, planning chief (situation status), and safety officer. You will gather the greatest amount of information from these personnel. You should also be aware of their roles on the incident.

One way to gather and organize information quickly at the scene is through the use of an information work sheet. The work sheet identifies information needed by the media. When you arrive on the scene, fill in the available information and disseminate it to the media.

EXTERNAL GATHERING OF DATA

The organization itself should not be the only source for information. A number of outside resources are also helpful. Gathering information begins with establishing networks and relationships. As the PIO, you will find that you have a greater

Figure 6.2 *Courtesy of Oklahoma City (Oklahoma) Fire Department.*

opportunity to establish networks than others within the department. Building bridges between your organization and other organizations, such as civic organizations, government agencies, associated fire related organizations, hospitals, churches, and schools, opens a lot of opportunities for information. If a working relationship cannot be established with an organizations' leadership, perhaps there are individuals within the organization who would be willing to network and share information.

The media is another external resource for information. Established relationships with members of the media prove to be beneficial. They typically are willing to render assistance, especially if it improves their opportunity for a story. Possible resources within the media include the media representatives, the assignment desk, and television station helicopters. You can best use these resources if you have developed relationships with them before the incident (see Chapter 5).

SUMMARY

Gathering information should be a vital part of what you do as the public information officer. Developing a strong network to use as a resource for gathering information is imperative. This network is developed through the ongoing positive relationships within the department and within the community. The positive relationships should be nourished and maintained. This will prove to be an asset when gathering information and disseminating it to the general public.

Chapter 7
Getting Information to the Media

The media is the best avenue for getting information to the public. The media reaches most communities every day. In larger cities, the media is going strong 24 hours a day. As a PIO, one of your jobs is to furnish department or emergency information to the media in a timely manner and in a format that can be used easily. This chapter provides you with tips on how to successfully provide your story to the media in a usable format.

There are three different approaches to providing information to the media. These approaches are referred to as the news release or press release, the media advisory, and direct contact with the media. Each approach is described below.

NEWS RELEASE

The *news release*, also known as a press release, is used to provide the

> ### BREAKING NEWS
>
> Many emergencies that face the incident commander can be more effectively mitigated through the use of the media. Evacuations, hazardous materials incidents, major road closures, floods, and other incidents which have widespread community impact can often be more effectively controlled with the media as a partner. The PIO can quickly release key information about the incident, and the media can release the alert to the public. No other communication tool has as wide of coverage as the collective power of the media. Building effective networks that can be accessed 24 hours a day will aid you in reaching the community.

media with information in a ready-to-use news story format. There are several different kinds of stories that you will want to put into a news release. Each type of story has a different focus and is used for a specific purpose. The types of stories are summarized below:

- *Human interest.* The human interest story focuses on events with an emotional, interpersonal appeal. Rescue stories, stories about firefighters providing special care to a citizen, etc., are appropriate for the news release format.

- *Investigation.* The investigation story provides information on an investigation including cause, fire loss, and details of the prosecution of arsonists. Remember, when releasing information regarding an investigation, you must consider the legal and ongoing investigation issues associated with the incident.

- *Incident summary.* This story provides the details on an emergency incident. It includes such facts as number of units responding, response times, cause, fire loss, and status of the residents or businesses.

- *Medical.* This story is similar to the incident summary except that it involves EMS incidents. There are legal issues associated with the release of medical information.

- *Department policy issue.* This story involves issues related to department policies and procedures. This specific type of story can be controversial and will typically require coordination with department leaders and legal counsel.

- *Educational.* The educational story involves information on fire and/or life safety behaviors and attitudes. Generally, this type of story provides the public with information on how to prevent or protect oneself from injury or fire.

Parts of the News Release

The news release has two parts: the heading and the body. The *heading* generally identifies the subject of the news release, the date the news release is being disseminated, the point of contact at the fire department, and when the news release can be used. Examples are shown in Figures 7.1 and 7.2.

The *body* or content of the news release contains the actual story that you want to get to the public. The story is written in the same style as a newspaper story. The story should be concise and easy to read. Also, the news release should be double-spaced and be on department letterhead. It must be free of grammar and spelling errors.

The story begins with a heading or title of the story. Think of this as the headline for the story. The title should summarize the meaning of the story. For example, let's say that your department was able to save a child involved in a car crash because of the quick actions of the rescue crew. You want to make sure that the headline captures the importance of the rescue. Your headline might read: "**Quick Action by Rescue Crew Saves Young Child.**" This headline would certainly catch the attention of both the media and the public.

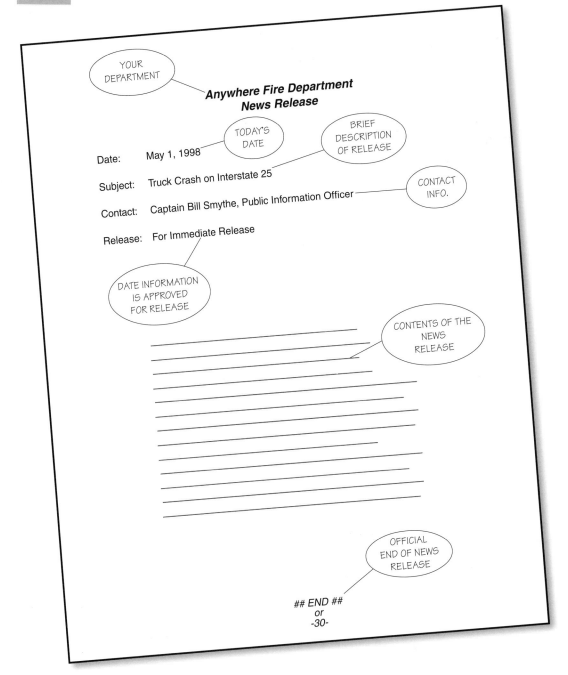

Figure 7.1 A news release should contain the above components. The importance of clear and accurate information cannot be overemphasized. A full-size copy of this document can be found on the disk included with the book.

City of Phoenix
FIRE DEPARTMENT
CORPORATE COMMUNICATIONS

Winner of the
Carl Bertelsmann
Prize

NEWS FOR IMMEDIATE RELEASE

Contact: Chief Bob Khan   495-7399

The Phoenix Fire Department recently honored two "pet protectors" with Official Commendations for their life saving efforts.

"Chance" a rottweiler, awoke his owners by barking, notifying them of a house fire across the street. This allowed them to alert their sleeping neighbors, certainly saving them from perishing in the fire.

Mary Beth Fisher, 11, was riding as an observer with her Fire Captain father, when they responded to a house fire. Mary Beth assisted in resuscitation of two dogs and a cat, allowing "Taz," one of the dogs, to survive.

These two special heroes, a dog that saved a family of humans and a little girl who saved a dog, received their Official Commendations at a Fire House ceremony.

150 South 12th Street, Phoenix, Arizona 85034 · 602-262-6910

Figure 7.2 An example of a news release sent out by the Phoenix Fire Department. A full-size copy of this document can be found on the disk included with the book.

The first paragraph of the story is the most important. It should contain a summary of the story and should hook the reader's interest in the story. Why? If the reader just reads the first paragraph, he or she will get the basics of the story. A rule used by newspaper journalists is that the most important parts of a story are at the beginning. As the story in a newspaper progresses, the importance of the information decreases. This allows the editor to cut the length of the story from the bottom without compromising the story. If your first paragraph contains the most important part of the story in a summary manner, the reader will get the information even if the rest of the story is cut by the editor or never read.

Although the big sensational stories will receive lots of coverage, not every news release you send to the media will be used. Routine stories that have value often end up on the last page or, unfortunately, on the edit room floor. A story that gets printed, even if it is one paragraph in the news brief section, is better than no story at all. By writing the news release in the proper format, with the most important information at the beginning, you will improve your chances of getting at least part of the story published or broadcast.

Back to the first paragraph of the news release. The paragraph should summarize the "who, what, when, where, and why" of the story. The reader should be able to read the first paragraph and get the basic idea about the story.

For example, let's build on the rescue of the young child by your rescue crew. The first paragraph in your news release might read something like this:

Jane Doe, a seven-year-old from Anywhere, was skillfully rescued from a wrecked car Saturday evening by firefighters from Anywhere Fire Department. The car

in which she was riding was hit by a drunk driver, and she became trapped. Firefighters from Rescue 1 were able to cut her out of the car in only two minutes. She was transported to Anywhere Hospital with serious injuries. There were no other injuries as a result of the crash.

NEWS RELEASE TIPS

1. Keep them short. Provide only the most important information to keep the story interesting. If the reporter wants more specific information, he or she can contact you and get a follow-up interview.

2. Only use news releases for valid stories. If you consistently send news releases that are not worthy of the public, the media will eventually not pay attention to any of your releases, even the good ones.

3. Get to know the needs and preferences of your local media and then compose your releases in that fashion.

4. When you can, include quotes from decision makers and those involved in the incidents and the stories. The public loves to read about the human interest part of emergency services.

5. Only put information in your news release that you know without a doubt is accurate and factual. Once you have sent it out, it is very difficult to retrieve and change.

6. Ask at least one other person to proofread the news release before disseminating it to the media.

7. When sending out a news release, make sure that it goes to all the local media. Failure to send it to all media may be perceived as preferential treatment and can cause mistrust and hurt relationships with the media.

8. Remember that news does have a usable life. Old news is seldom used. You need to get your news release to the media in time for their news deadline. The best way to do this is by fax or e-mail. If you live in a small community, you may even deliver it yourself. Avoid sending it by mail as it may not get there in time to be good news.

The remaining paragraphs in the news release should provide more detailed information. Remember, you are writing to the public, so it should contain information and details that are interesting for the general public or the target audience you are trying to reach.

It is also helpful to include one or more quotes from key officials and personnel. This tends to add a human perspective to the stories. Quotes from citizens who are praising the efforts of the department are especially beneficial. If you are going to use a quote, make sure that you get the quote verbatim from the person. Only put actual quotes in the news release.

A news release should be no more than three pages long, and it is best if it is one or two pages. If there is more information than can be fitted into three pages, put the extra information into another news release as a separate but related story. At the end of the news release use ##END## or -30- to indicate the end of the news release.

MEDIA ADVISORIES

The media advisory is a means for you to communicate important information about department events to the media. Unlike the news release, the target audience of the media advisory is the media rather than the public. An example of a media advisory is shown in Figure 7.3.

For example, if you wanted to announce a news conference, you would use a media advisory to notify the media. You would also use a media advisory to notify the media of community events that you would like announced. These could include open houses, neighborhood meetings, public education events, etc.

The media advisory is written in much the same format as the news release. It should be written on letterhead and should

150 S. 12th Street
Phoenix, AZ 85034-2301
(602) 534-0953

PHOENIX FIRE DEPARTMENT
HONORS "PET PROTECTORS"

MEDIA ADVISORY

Contact: Bob Khan   (phone number)
           pager   (phone number)

WHAT: The Phoenix Fire Department is proud to bestow *Official Commendations to two special heroes...a dog who saved a family of humans and a little girl who worked hard to save two dogs and a cat.* "Chance", a rottweiler, awoke his owners with an unusual bark alerting them to a *house fire across the street.* Had he and his owners not notified its sleeping occupants, *they would have perished. Mary Beth Fisher, 11,* was riding as an observer with her father, Captain Dan Fisher, when they responded to a house fire. Mary Beth *quickly assisted in the resusci tation of dogs "Carmel" and "Taz" and cat "Spaz",* although only "Taz" survived. The Phoenix Fire Department is proud of the quick actions of both "Chance" and Mary Beth. People can *learn more* about saving all members of their family by attending *"Survival Saturday for Pets and People"* this Saturday.

WHEN: Friday, August 28, 1998
             3:00 p.m.

WHERE: Phoenix Fire Station 9
             330 E. Fairmont

Contact on Site: Captain Chris Ketterer
                     pager: (phone number)

Figure 7.3 An example of a media advisory released by the Phoenix Fire Department. A full-size copy of this document can be found on the disk included with the book.

be double-spaced. It must be neat and be free from grammar and spelling errors.

The heading of the media advisory is the same as the news release with one exception. The media advisory does not have a "Release" line as the information is not being released.

The body of the media advisory is basically a message to the media. It provides detailed information on the event or other issue. If it is an event, you should identify the importance of the event; why it is newsworthy or why the media should attend; the location, time, and date; and who will be attending. Remember, the media is getting requests for stories from all different sorts of organizations and agencies. They will cover those events and stories that appear to have the greatest appeal and value to the public.

Emergency Alert System

In January 1997, the Federal Communications Commission (FCC) activated the Emergency Alert System (EAS). This new system replaced the Emergency Broadcast System. EAS is an industry government response to a Presidential Statement of Requirements, providing the Commander and Chief the capability to address the nation during emergencies. At the national level, only the President can activate the EAS.

The EAS transmits national, state, and local warning messages that can be used to notify you and your family and friends about emergency situations. The system is designed to automatically break regular programming to provide guidance to your specific viewing or listening area. The EAS uses a digital system that allows broadcast stations, cable systems, participating satellite companies, and other services to send and receive emergency information. This provides the public with timely emergency lifesaving messages.

The new system is designed to turn on new, specially equipped consumer products, such as car radios, pagers, and other devices, to receive an EAS alert and warning. Contact your local station to determine what emergency messages will be transmitted. Some stations may also transmit in foreign languages common to their area. You may contact the FCC's National Call Center at 1-888-Call-FCC or contact them via their web site at www.fcc.gov/cib/eas.

MEDIA ADVISORY TIPS

1. If you are inviting the media to a public event, send out a media advisory two weeks in advance and then again two days prior to the event.

2. Make sure that the information you provide in the news release is detailed enough to get the interest of the media. Emphasize the benefit to the public from the media responding to the advisory.

3. If dignitaries or elected officials are participating in fire department events, list them in the advisory. Many times celebrities will draw the media to an event.

4. If you are cooperating with other agencies on an event, coordinate the dissemination of the media advisories. It is best to only send advisories from one organization so that the media is not confused about conflicting information or multiple advisories.

5. When you send out an advisory, send it to all the local media. See #7 in News Release Tips.

DIRECT CONTACT

One of the best ways to get information to the media is by contacting reporters directly with the information. This approach requires that you have a positive relationship with the

Figure 7.4 One of the best ways to get information to the media is by contacting reporters directly with the information. *Courtesy of Oklahoma City (Oklahoma) Fire Department.*

reporters. It should also be used only when you can provide the information adequately and consistently over the phone or with an interview. When you contact a reporter directly with a story, be prepared to send a news release with additional information, facts, figures, etc.

Direct contact is also a good method for following up on a news release. While you do not want to be a "pest," there are times when you want to ensure that the news release was received. Remember that most newsrooms and city desks are busy places, and faxes and news releases can get lost. Do not lose a good story because of a lost news release.

SUMMARY

A key element in effective public information is remembering that the media holds the keys to getting your message out to the public. The best tools you have to accomplish this task are well-written and timely news releases and media advisories. When used appropriately, these tools will enhance your chances of being published or aired by the media.

Chapter 8
The Interview

An *interview* is an exchange of information in which the message goes to all the readers, all the listeners, and all the viewers to whom that reporter provides information. Each type of interview has a unique process. Therefore, the PIO should have an orientation to each type of interview (television, radio, or print media) and an understanding of how each should be addressed. During any type of interview, the public information officer provides the link between the fire department and the community. The interview can either strengthen or weaken the

Figure 8.1 Interviews are an excellent opportunity for departmental visibility. Take these opportunities to have the departmental insignia visible during interviews. *Courtesy of Phoenix (Arizona) Fire Department.*

credibility of the organization in the eyes of the public. It is essential that the public information officer does not distract the viewer from the message by his or her personal verbal mannerisms, dress, or actions. Regardless of the type of interview, the following considerations for print, radio, and TV interviews must be applied in order for them to be successful.

PRINT

The most important characteristic of a print interview is that it must be detail-oriented. Details help the reader see and understand the point of the interview. They are also important because the story may not run when the event is still clearly in the minds of the readers. You must rebuild the event, tell the story, and recreate the mental picture for anyone who reads it. This is best accomplished by using supporting documents and quotes. There must be a lot of interaction between the

Print Interview Preparation

- Prepare for a longer interview with more details needed by the reporter. Prepare for an interview that may take longer than a radio or TV interview.

- Make sure that the environment is comfortable.

- Have facts assembled.

- When appropriate, provide diagrams and photos to enhance the story.

- Provide access to other personnel who may be asked to contribute to the story.

- Be specific about critical issues, and consider providing written reference materials for technical information.

- Plan for a photo opportunity session.

- Provide ideas for sidebar stories.

interviewer and the interviewee during the course of a print interview. During this interaction, it is important to make an effort to repeat key information often and state it in different ways. It is often helpful and to your benefit to provide photographs with the article.

RADIO

A radio interview lends itself to an even different set of rules in order for it to be successful. The radio medium is often a fast-paced environment, and this is often the way that the interview must be conducted. This is not to say that you should feel rushed or give incomplete answers. But rather than focusing on details and repetition, such as you do in the print interview, your answers should come in the way of sound bites.

Link your comments to the key point that you want to make during the interview. Remember to make your answers

Radio Interview Preparation

- Get the key point across quickly. Talk in sound bites.

- Monitor local talk shows, and be prepared to call in with pertinent information.

- Be prepared for anything during live radio interviews.

- Be prepared to give incident interviews over the phone.

- Inform citizens of critical public safety events, such as evacuations and storm warnings.

- Provide written reference materials before the interview when possible.

- Use your voice to convey the appropriate emotion — use descriptive terms.

- Plant seeds for other stories when talking to radio reporters.

descriptive and as to the point as possible. Focus your attention on the reporter as you would do in a print interview. Do not let the microphone distract you. Your voice is the most important feature in a radio interview. Make every effort to be animated and use inflection. Remember that reporters have difficulty asking the "perfect" question to elicit the relevant information. Be assertive in giving the relevant information, even if the question doesn't ask for that exact response. The reporter will have the opportunity to re-ask the question if you failed to address the key components of the original question. You should also be prepared to tie key concepts together so that it is difficult to edit critical messages. For example, if you said, "Let me give you the three reasons why you shouldn't use gasoline as a cleaning solution." As you can imagine, editing reasons number two and three would generate many phone calls to the station.

TELEVISION

Unlike the radio, your voice is not the only focus of your audience — they can also see you. The interviewer may give you guidance on proper techniques to use or not use in a studio interview. It is critical that you also provide a good backdrop for TV interviews. Placing the incident or your apparatus behind the interview may provide for some additional visual marketing in addition to the message you are delivering. Having your apparatus clearly marked is a marketing advantage both on and off the camera.

GENERAL GUIDELINES FOR AN EFFECTIVE INTERVIEW

While each form of media carries guidelines that are specific to its form, some guidelines are consistent with all forms of media. Use the following guidelines to improve media interviews:

Television Interview Preparation

- Provide opportunities for active, stimulating background video and natural sound.

- Ensure that the department logo or name is visible in the picture.

- Keep it concise (sound bites are typically 20 seconds or less).

- Provide a large amount of physical space for equipment.

- Look at the reporter and not the camera.

- Dress appropriately for the interview situation.

- Project your voice and maintain correct posture.

- Stand still and use controlled gestures.

- Be prepared for a live interview.

- Expect multiple interviews in a short time frame.

- Make operational personnel accessible to reporters on the scene when appropriate.

Before an Interview

- *Be prepared.* Review all pertinent information before the interview. Have reference notes. Inquire about what questions will be asked.

- *Be newsworthy, factual, and correct.* Check and double-check information before releasing it to the media. **Never deceive the public.**

- *Keep both your emotions and intellect in check.* What you say is just as important as how you say it. Emotions can often be evident, regardless of the actual spoken words. This is not to say that you should not show appropriate emotion. If you believe you may have difficulty controlling your emotions, delay the interview or have an associate step in for you. The motivation for emotional reactions are often situational and difficult to communicate to the viewing public. It is best to remain professional and calm although empathy is always appropriate.

- *Anticipate what will happen during the course of the interview.*

- *Prepare for the interview, but do not memorize what you are going to say.*

General Tips for Success

- Be assertive in the interview, and communicate your key points.

- Be proactive with story ideas. Don't wait for the media to come to you.

- Prepare in advance for major emergencies.

- Tell your side of the story early regarding controversial issues.

- Tell the truth — don't deceive.

- Do your best to meet the informational needs of the media during the interview.

- Stay current on department statistics, services, and policies.

- Know your department's position.

- Seize opportunities for teachable moments.

- Promote fire and life safety behaviors and attitudes.

- Follow up on commitments made during interviews.

During the Interview

- *Portray a professional image:*

  — Use appropriate verbal and nonverbal communication.

  — Avoid chewing gum, smoking, or eating.

  — Act confident.

  — Look the reporter in the eyes.

  — Maintain a positive attitude.

- *Use nongender specific terms.* For example, use "firefighter" (not fireman) and "staffing" (not manning). It will help you during an interview if you use nongender specific terms in your day-to-day language. Interviews are often pressure performances, and we often revert to our daily patterns when stressed. Developing good habits during daily business will often help you avoid mistakes when the pressure is on.

- *Plan the points you want to make.* State the most important points or conclusions at the start of the interview. Single-sentence summaries are helpful.

- *Choose your words carefully.* Use language everyone understands. Avoid fire service jargon and technical terms.

- *Act natural.* Do not be pretentious, be yourself.

- *Project an image of credibility that will reflect well on your department.*

- *Always assume that you are "on record."* Interviewers often record your conversations which can be used publicly.

- *Avoid saying "No comment." It invites speculation. As always, it is okay to respond "I do not know."*

- *Do not repeat a reporter's negative or leading words in your answer.*

- *Avoid responding to hypothetical situations.*

- *Keep the interview on track.*

- *Assign no blame and avoid criticism.*

- *Develop an offensive strategy for controversial issues and prepare to defend your position.*

- *Give credit where credit is due when discussing an issue.* Make sure to recognize all parties that have been involved.

SUMMARY

The general public may judge departmental activities as a success or failure by how the media portrays the event. How the PIO interviews will also have a great influence on this outcome. The PIO is a representative of the department in the eyes of the media and the general public.

Chapter 9
Scene Management

During an emergency situation, the incident commander remains responsible for managing public information. However, the incident commander may delegate the public information function when needed as designated in the department's SOPs. Therefore, the PIO is an essential part of the Incident Management System (IMS) and is directly accountable to the incident commander. The PIO serves as a point of contact between the incident commander and the media. This allows for a clear and direct dissemination of information.

It is the PIO's responsibility to gather, prepare, and provide information to the media. The PIO is crucial in relaying important facts of the incident and its impact upon the community (Figure 9.1). The PIO sees that the media gets the story it needs safely, quickly, and efficiently. The goal is to help the media put together an accurate, understandable, fact-filled account of the emergency and to make certain that reporters are safe and not in the way of those who are attempting to secure and manage the scene. This is also an opportunity for the PIO to give the community insight into the men and women who serve within the department.

Expanded Organization
Incident Management - **Major Incident**

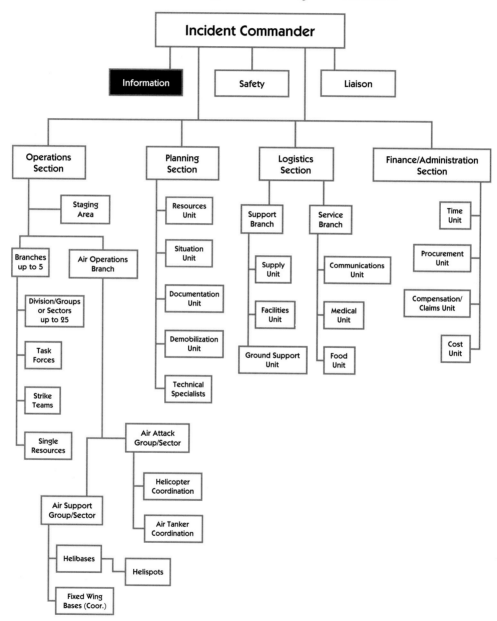

Figure 9.1 The role of the PIO is important to the overall operation of the incident. Note that the PIO reports directly to the Incident Commander.

As the PIO, you must understand what your duties are on the scene and what the expectations are from the media, the general public, and the department in which you serve. Specifically within this chapter, we look at the means for working with the media on the incident scene and useful tools to use in this process.

In the event of an emergency, reporters do not care whether a fire department handling the emergency is large or small. They simply need accurate, timely information. Big stories can occur in small places. If the department experiences infrequent contact with the press, it is all the more important to have a plan prepared. Preplanning is a key element in establishing successful operations. Do not be lulled into a false sense of complacency.

PHASES OF SCENE MANAGEMENT

The size and intensity of a scene will vary greatly from incident to incident; however, there is a consistent pattern to its phases. The phases of scene management are scene assessment and media scene management.

Scene Assessment

Assessing the emergency scene is one of the first steps in the process of sizing up an incident. This applies to the PIO as it does to all officers involved in the scene. The PIO performs several steps in the initial scene assessment:

Step 1: Receives initial information when dispatched and listens to the operational radio traffic upon arrival to the scene. The PIO learns a great deal about the situation through this information.

Step 2:   Reports to the Incident Commander (IC) for a briefing on the situation and receives instructions. Uses a media work sheet to record the observed and gathered information about the incident. This work sheet basically anticipates questions the media will ask. (See Figure 9.2)

Media Scene Management

It is imperative that your system be staffed with a PIO who can arrive ahead of or shortly after the media. This facilitates the timely establishment of a media area before the media becomes "spread out" around the incident.

Upon arrival of the incident, the PIO should receive a briefing from the IC and make a recommendation for the location of a media area for the release of information. The media area should be located in a safe area that provides an optimal view of the incident. The media area should be separate from the general public and be monitored by the PIO. Be sure to provide an adequate buffer from the incident management function as to not interfere with those functions. Adequate space and the functionality of the media area are critical to effectively service the needs of the media. The PIO should consider the strategic placement of the media area to facilitate interesting backdrops to photographs and video shots. You should always strive to provide as good an environment as possible. You should perform the following when managing the media scene:

- Alert the media to your location.

- Use identifying vests and attire to mark information staff.

- Let the reporters know when to check for updates of the breaking story — perhaps on the quarter hour or

PUBLIC INFORMATION WORKSHEET — Page 1

PUBLIC INFORMATION WORKSHEET

DATE: _____   Fire _____ EPS _____ Hzmt _____

TIMES: Dispatched: _____ On Scene: _____ Controlled: _____
Tapped: _____ Cleared Scene: _____
Alarms: 2nd _____ 3rd _____ 4th _____
Zone: 1 _____ 2 _____ 3 _____ 4 _____

DISPATCH: Reason Dispatched: _____
Address: _____
Occupancy: _____
Owner: _____

OCCUPANCY: Residential Structure: _____
Multi-family: _____
Commercial: _____
Business/Function: _____

APPARATUS: Engines   _____   Aid   _____   Cmd Cars _____
Ladders   _____   Hzmt   _____   Medic   _____
Amb   _____   PD   _____   WNG   _____
DOE   _____   EPA   _____   PUD   _____
RC   _____   Support _____

MUTUAL AID DEPARTMENTS/RESOURCES: _____
_____
_____
_____

SITUATION ENCOUNTERED/ACTION TAKEN: _____
_____
_____
_____
_____
_____
_____
_____
_____
_____
_____
_____
_____
_____
_____

Figure 9.2 Examples of PIO work sheets for varying incidents. A full-size copy of these documents can be found on the disk included with the book.

PUBLIC INFORMATION WORKSHEET — Page 2

SPECIAL HAZARDS/ACCOMPLISHMENTS/RECOMMENDATIONS: _____

_____
_____
_____
_____
_____
_____
_____
_____
_____
_____
_____
_____
_____
_____

INJURIES/FATALITIES: Civilian (C) _____   Firefighter (FF) _____

Name	Sex	Age	Injury	Where Taken

DAMAGE: _____

_____
_____
_____

$ ESTIMATE: _____

CAUSE: _____

_____
_____
_____

PUBLIC EDUCATION MESSAGE: _____

_____
_____
_____

SMOKE DETECTORS: Installed _____   Operating _____

Figure 9.2 Continued

HAZARDOUS MATERIALS INCIDENT WORKSHEET — Page 1

HAZARDOUS MATERIALS INCIDENT WORKSHEET

DATE: _____ Fire _____ EPS _____ Hzmt _____

TIMES: Dispatched: _____ On Scene: _____ Controlled: _____
Tapped: _____ Cleared Scene: _____
Alarms: 2nd _____ 3rd _____ 4th _____
Zone: 1 _____ 2 _____ 3 _____ 4 _____

DISPATCH: Reason Dispatched: _____
Address: _____
Occupancy: _____
Owner: _____

OCCUPANCY: Residential Structure: _____
Multi-family: _____
Commercial: _____
Business/Function: _____

APPARATUS: Engines _____ Aid _____ Cmd Cars _____
Ladders _____ Hzmt _____ Medic _____
Amb _____ PD _____ WNG _____
DOE _____ EPA _____ PUD _____
RC _____ Support _____

MUTUAL AID DEPARTMENTS/RESOURCES: _____
_____
_____
_____

SITUATION ENCOUNTERED/ACTION TAKEN: _____
_____
_____
_____
_____
_____
_____
_____
_____
_____
_____

Quantity & State: _____
Product Use: _____

INJURIES: _____
_____
_____

Figure 9.2 Continued

HAZARDOUS MATERIALS INCIDENT WORKSHEET — Page 2

COMPANY/INDIVIDUAL NAME (ADDRESS IF DIFFERENT THAN LOCATION): _____

_____

_____

_____

PRODUCT NAME: _____

SPECIAL CONSIDERATIONS - FIRE/WATER/AIR/HEALTH: _____

_____

_____

_____

ROAD CLOSURES/EVACUATIONS: _____

_____

CONTAINMENT/CONTROL: _____

_____

ENVIRONMENTAL HAZARDS: _____

_____

DECONTAMINATION: _____

_____

CLEAN-UP: _____

_____

FOLLOW-UP: _____

_____

Figure 9.2 Continued

PIO WORKSHEET — Page 1

PIO WORKSHEET

Address _____ TOA _____ Arrival _____

Owner/Resident _____ Age _____

Alarm # _____ Type of Structure _____ Units _____

Unit ____ Arrival ____ Command _____

Unit ____ Arrival ____ Safety _____

Unit ____ Arrival ____ Liaison _____

Unit ____ Arrival ____ Operations _____

Unit ____ Arrival ____ City Safety _____

Unit ____ Arrival ____ City Public Relations _____

Unit ____ Arrival ____ Medical _____

Unit ____ Arrival ____ Investigations _____

MEDIA WORKSHEET

Unit _____ Name _____

Unit _____ Name _____

Unit _____ Name _____

Unit _____ Name _____

Unit _____ Name _____

Unit _____ Name _____

Unit _____ Name _____

Unit _____ Name _____

_____ _____

CAUSE OF FIRE

Location of Ignition _____

Cause of Ignition _____

Contributing Factors _____

Smoke Detector Present: Yes _____   No _____

Operate: Yes _____   No _____

Awoke Residents: Yes _____   No _____

Comments of Investigator _____

_____

_____

_____

_____

_____

_____

_____

_____

Figure 9.2 Continued

PIO WORKSHEET — Page 2

INJURIES

Name _____ Age _____ To/By _____
Injury _____
Name _____ Age _____ To/By _____
Injury _____
Other Information _____
_____
_____
_____

AGENCY SUPPORT

Agency _____ POC _____
Type of Support _____
Agency _____ POC _____
Type of Support _____
Comments by PIO_____
_____
_____
_____
_____
_____
_____
_____
_____
_____
_____
_____
_____
_____
_____
_____
_____
_____
_____
_____
_____
_____

Figure 9.2 Continued

the half hour. Once you determine the meeting times, stick to them whether you have new information or not.

- Give the reporters the ground rules up front. Identify the safe and unsafe areas.

THE MEDIA POOL

A media pool is needed when a scene requires limited access, and all media cannot be brought to the scene. In these circumstances, it may be necessary for the PIO to establish a media pool. The PIO will establish which representatives of the media, such as a photographer, reporter, or both, will be part of the media pool. The media selects the person who will provide the information for the collective body. The story is then shared with all media present. This is also an effective tool to use with scene photography. Some tips to follow with pool reporters are the following:

Guidelines for Locating your Media Area

- Set up in a safe area.
- Provide optimal view of the incident.
- Separate from the public.
- Make sure that it does not interfere with command functions.
- Allow adequate space for media.
- Clearly mark the area.
- Monitor the area.

- *Allow the media to select its own representative.* The individual who represents the media should be someone in which they hold with a great deal of professional credibility and integrity. As the PIO, you should not be the one to pick the individual. It could appear that you do not trust the decisions of the media, and you may not select the most qualified individual.

- *Be very specific about the rules and requirements.* Remember that special circumstances are involved if you are using a pool reporter or photographer. The reporter should have a clear understanding of what he or she can and cannot do. He or she should understand that safety is the reason why these rules are necessary.

- *Develop and share expectations.* This should be in conjunction with the previous guidelines. The circumstances for having a pool photographer or reporter are for logistical and safety reasons. As the PIO, you should inform the person what your expectations are for him or her, and the person should clearly understand them.

- *Ensure that you understand and handle the needs of the media who will be remaining in the media sector.* You have an ethical responsibility to ensure that some of the media are not "scooped" because of the pool process. Developing a system in which you can ensure that all members of the media on scene will be able to access the same information will alleviate any frustration and the appearance of favoritism.

- *Do everything you can to ensure the safety of the pool reporter.* As the PIO, you should do everything you can to ensure the safety of the pool reporter or photographer. Always maintain that his or her safety is your first priority.

PROVIDING MEDIA TOURS

As the PIO, you should attempt to provide media access tours as soon as possible following incident stabilization. The following are considerations for media access tours:

- *Provide appropriate gear for the media.* As was previously mentioned, this provides an opportunity for safety and accountability for members of the media. Again, safety is your utmost priority.

- *Develop and implement a program for media identification.* This type of program facilitates many of the areas that we have discussed and encourages a better relationship with the media. This is an organized means for establishing your expectations of the media before the incident. Identification of the media eliminates much confusion during the incident. (For additional information, see the "Phoenix Fire Department's Certified Fire Journalist Academy" in Chapter 5.)

- *Coordinate the tour with the incident commander and, when applicable, the operations section chief or incident safety officer.* As with all activities on the scene, the incident commander and safety officer should be aware of the events taking place. This improves the safety aspect of the tour and removes any confusion that may result from lack of communication. For more information on legal issues associated with this, see Chapter 3.

SUMMARY

The role of the PIO in the IMS structure is critical. He or she must understand and observe the command structure, the polices and procedures of the department, and the responsibilities involved when working with the media at a scene. The duties of the PIO are not simple and must be planned and developed in conjunction with departmental policies and procedures. If the PIO does not have the operational experience, he or she must have a clear understanding of the operational function. The PIO is imperative to the success of any incident operation.

Chapter 10

Multiagency Operations: Information Operations at the Large Incident

Today as a PIO, you are more likely than ever to work in a multiagency operation. Many incidents require multiagency cooperation to adequately protect citizens and the environment. Multiagency response differs in a number of ways. As the PIO, you must understand the variance in response and have a comprehension of how these incidents may differ from your normal departmental operations. Typically, multiagency responses are longer in length and of a

Figure 10.1 Multiple agency responses have different requirements that must be understood and recognized on the scene. *Courtesy of Oklahoma City (Oklahoma) Fire Department.*

larger scale. This type of response requires a much greater need for resources and personnel, which many departments do not have. Having a variety of agencies providing the resources can be an enormous asset to the immediate responding department.

Multiple-agency responses have different requirements that must be understood and recognized on the scene. Different agencies may have varying standard operating procedures to follow and varying means in which they handle an incident. Their procedures and policies may conflict with your departmental policies and operations. Depending on the level and type of incident, there may be agencies from federal, state, county, private, city, borough, province, special districts, or private industry. Each brings a unique purpose and responsibility. Different agencies provide unique resources that can positively enhance outcomes. For this cooperation to be effective, the participating agencies must understand each other's responsibilities, resources, and needs.

As the PIO, you must understand the diversity among the agencies responding and how this impacts your responsibilities on the scene. Other agencies may have PIOs established and that person has the same commitment to his or her organization as you do to yours. There may be competition for media time as each person promotes the agency he or she represents. Attempts by you and your fellow PIOs to lessen the competition for media time will alleviate a great deal of frustration and lessen the opportunity for release of conflicting information. Much of this can be resolved through clear communication and cooperation between agencies. Early cooperation and a strong communication system between PIOs will help to eliminate problems in collection, dissemination, and distribution of information.

PIO PLANNING AND OPERATIONS

The initial step in establishing a strong relationship with the PIOs of other agencies starts before the incident. It begins by meeting and establishing a relationship with the PIOs of other agencies and neighboring departments. Understanding the individuals and their expectations can assist in an effective working relationship on the scene. The actual incident is not the optimum time to get to know the PIOs with whom you will be working.

An excellent opportunity to begin this relationship is through training and drills. Regular training together not only builds relationships but provides opportunities for development and improvement of on-scene operations. An established joint-training program provides for continued team development and team competency. This would be an excellent opportunity to develop Joint Information Center (JIC) operating procedures. Many multiagency responses fail because of lack of planning and preparation by all agencies involved. Coordinating the communication efforts of all agencies and their technologies, such as radios, computers, software, printers, and so forth, eliminates confusion and the overlapping of precious resources.

Once all this has been developed, ongoing training should be implemented for all related staff to provide continued proficiency in each area. Your plan should address the following:

- JIC structure
- Operating guidelines
- Technology needs
- Staffing pattern
- Facility needs
- JIC function/roles communicated to media

Establishing a unified public information function may be very beneficial. In fact, many laws, policies, and agreements require a joint information effort. Joint decision making allows the involvement of all or selected PIOs in the decision-making process.

USING A JOINT INFORMATION CENTER

The true test of your development of policies and procedures, training, and preparation comes when the incident occurs. In essence, it is "the time of truth." The initiation of the JIC should be as close to the beginning of the incident as possible. Having a strong communication center established at the beginning of the incident results in a well-facilitated line of communication throughout the incident. This prevents a great deal of frustration on the part of the media, the general public, all agencies involved, and your department. Each JIC participant should obtain prior approval from his or her agency before participating in the public information team. The following steps will assist you in the operation of a strong Joint Information Center.

TIPS FOR A SUCCESSFUL JIC

- Coordinate JIC operations with Incident Command.
- Develop an information strategy which includes an agenda.
- Make sure that the media understands how to access information from the JIC.
- Distribute and share decisions and information with other PIOs.
- Prepare and use JIC letterhead identifying the agencies involved in the incident.

> ## TECHNOLOGY AS A TOOL
>
> The following technologies may be used to improve the efficiency and effectiveness of the JIC operation:
>
> - Computers and printers
> - Fax machines (separate incoming and outgoing Fax machines)
> - Radios and cell phones
> - Computer modem and Internet access
> - Split-screen televisions
> - Satellite uplinks and downlinks
> - Videotape recorders for recording television broadcasts

"TURF" ISSUES

Each agency responding to the incident brings its own goals and responsibilities. This can be an asset or a hindrance to the incident depending on interagency relationships. Preplanning may resolve potential conflicts before they occur. Issues such as competition for media exposure, personal opinion, and differences in levels of authority and jurisdiction can create divisions within the team. Be prepared to defend your role and the actions of your department; however, do so with respect to the others' roles and responsibilities. If the issue cannot be resolved within the team, then it must be addressed through the appropriate channels and chain of command. Conflicts should be resolved quickly to avoid further team division and a loss of confidence and credibility with the public.

MEDIA BRIEFING

During large-scale emergencies, it will be necessary to conduct periodic news briefings to give current information to the media and to answer questions. The following are some tips for conducting successful media briefings:

- *Identify the media's needs.* Understanding what they are looking for and what information would be beneficial for them will be a great asset.

- *Set an agenda and schedule.* Having a clear and reasonable agenda and schedule will facilitate the transfer of information. Cooperatively set an agenda and a schedule with the media.

- *Be timely.* Simply establishing an agenda and schedule is not enough. As the PIO, you must meet the time frames set. This alleviates frustration and possible freelancing on the part of the media.

- *Respond quickly to changes in incident status.* Be prepared to notify the media of changes — both positive and negative — as they occur. It is more beneficial for you to be the one to provide incident status information than for the media to find out from other means.

- *Use a facilitator.* If resources allow, using a facilitator will free you to focus on the important issues surrounding the incident. Someone who can work as a liaison to meet any basic needs of the media will greatly enhance the department's image and create a positive working environment.

- *Identify the media involved.* As was previously discussed, an effective accountability system is necessary for record keeping and to eliminate any possible freelancing on the part of the media.

- *Provide access to senior officials.* While the PIO can be an excellent and the most effective resource, there may be times the information may need to come from the upper ranks. Be a facilitator in these situations — not a hindrance. This is a great opportunity for other members of the department to become familiar with the media.

- *Be aware of potential human interest stories.* The media can be used as a resource for your department as well as the information source for the public. Be on the lookout for human interest stories. Human interest stories provide an opportunity to make "household names" out of the men and women who serve your department and the community. Building a relationship between the individuals and the community can create a positive image for the department as a whole.

SUMMARY

Multiagency operations rely heavily on good coordination and communication among all agencies involved. A successful operation is one that is well-planned and organized. It is also outlined before, during, and after the incident. The benefactor of good communication, coordination, and cooperation is the public.

Chapter 11 News Conferences

News conferences are used when an agency needs to reach multiple media agencies through a focused, managed event. A major benefit of a news conference is that you are able to release information and directly answer questions posed by the media. It is important that you are properly prepared, understand the circumstances with which you are dealing, and successfully convey the message you want to the community. Refer to

Figure 11.1 *Courtesy of Oklahoma City (Oklahoma) Fire Department.*

Chapter 4, "The Media," for more information on what each type of media expects and needs to do its job. This information may be useful when preparing for a news conference.

PLANNING A NEWS CONFERENCE

The ability to conduct a proper news conference is based upon your ability to plan and organize information. Because you are the one coordinating the news conference, you should make every effort before the news conference to obtain vital information related to the news conference.

News Conference Preparation

Step 1: **Identify the need for a news conference.** Make sure that the issue or desired message is important and not trivial. Do not cry wolf.

Step 2: **Identify points to be addressed and create an agenda.** As PIO it is important for you to understand the issues that need to be addressed at the news conference. In cooperation with the media, set a specific start and end time.

You should have the following information available:

- Departmental statistics

- Incident statistics

- Related life-safety statistics

- Relevant national stories and statistics. There should be no reason for you to be caught off guard because of the lack of information.

- Spin-off stories that may be good follow-ups.

Step 3: **Identify and rehearse individual roles.** Review the agenda with the individuals who will be speaking. Make sure that each participant is aware of his or her role, comfortable with the information he or she is expected to provide, and informed about protocols.

Step 4: **Reconfirm with the media the time, location, and purpose of a news conference.** The Media Packet will also help ensure that correct information is provided to the media.

Tips for Conducting a News Conference

- Provide adequate electrical service for the media equipment.

- Minimize distractions, such as ringing phones, etc.

- Ask people to turn off pagers, phones, etc., (or set to vibrate mode) during the conference.

- Start your media conference by answering the questions that were unanswered during the last conference. This demonstrates attention to detail and will build confidence that questions will be addressed (which reduces probing follow-up questions).

- Hold a joint media conference if other agencies are involved.

- Schedule the starting time for the conference with attention toward media deadlines.

- If the number of television cameras exceeds your ability to accommodate them, ask the media to pool (share) a single camera.

- Save an area outside the conference area for live microwave towers to be set up.

SUMMARY

An important function of the public information officer is to have the ability to plan and conduct a news conference. The PIO needs to understand the benefits and purpose of the news conference being held. By understanding this need, he or she will be able to prepare an agenda that addresses the key points. The agenda should be easy to follow and maintain during the news conference. Following this agenda allows the PIO to manage the news conference so that he or she can accurately disseminate the pertinent information to the media.

Chapter 12

Reaching the Community

As the PIO for your department, you play an important role in reaching the community. You have the ability to positively or negatively shape the public's perception of the fire department. When you do your job more effectively, the community will have a more positive attitude toward the fire department. The following can help you reach members of your community:

- Public speaking engagements
- Community organizations
- Web site
- Intergovernmental relations
- Advertisement/mass media
- Internal communications

PUBLIC SPEAKING

Public speaking engagements enable you to get out and actually have face-to-face communication with members of your community — this is the most direct communication that you can have with the end users of your fire department's services. Public speaking allows you to interact with members of the community and receive feedback regarding your department.

Public speaking is an excellent tool for community relations. It can be used to promote a local or national cause in the fire service. The opportunity for public speaking arises regularly, and it is to your department's advantage to use whenever possible. Civic and fraternal organizations often use guest speakers. You can use this opportunity to reach the community.

Maintain a Source of Qualified Speakers

The PIO should not always be the individual who addresses the public. It is often a good idea to schedule other trained speakers to interact with members of the community. This provides a broader range of information that can be used. The PIO should develop a group of qualified speakers such as the fire chief, training officers, fire marshal, fire and life safety educators, and community experts who have associated expertise. It is important for the PIO to know his or her knowledge limitations and have resources within the department that can help get the necessary answers.

CAUTION: Remember that these speakers represent you and your organization. Before sending them out, it is essential that you ensure that they have the knowledge of the topic and speaking skills.

Understand your Audience

When speaking to a community organization (or any group for that matter), understanding the audience enhances your presentation. For example, if you are speaking to a school group, knowing the age allows you to focus the presentation toward that age group. The following are important factors to keep in mind when preparing for public speaking engagements:

- Select audience-appropriate topics and information.

- Understand the cultural and societal norms of the group

- Provide appropriate visual aids.

Prepare and Schedule Public Speaking Engagements

As the PIO, you represent the department to the general public. The quality of service that the department provides should also be reflected in your speaking. This comes from careful planning and thorough preparation. Keep the following important tasks in mind when preparing and arranging public speaking engagements:

- Make an effort to keep all commitments. Do not cancel unless it is absolutely necessary to do so. If you cannot attend, try to schedule someone else to speak in your place.

- Designate a contact person, whether it is you or someone else, so that organizations and media personnel can know how to contact you.

- Have current and timely information, both local and national, readily available so that preparation does not have to become all consuming.

COMMUNITY ORGANIZATIONS

Civic organizations are the central points of the community. As the public information officer, it is of key importance to network with these groups and form strong relationships. By doing

Figure 12.1 *Courtesy of Oklahoma City (Oklahoma) Fire Department.*

so, you are able to impact large numbers of key people within the community.

A helpful tool is to maintain an up-to-date list of the organizations that have a special relationship with your department, have contributed in the past, or have asked you to speak on previous occasions. This allows you to be proactive and suggest opportunities for joint efforts and activities. It is also helpful to have background information on the organization, which will help you focus your presentation on that organization's unique interest and issues. Your list should also include the charities in which you have given or aided in the past as well as ones that you may be able to contribute to in the future. This list of community organizations is available from most Chamber of Commerce or community service divisions of local government. You can maximize your contact with the community by doing the following:

- Understanding special relationships and how they work to help the department. Examples of these relationships can be the local Red Cross or the local school district.

- Knowing neighborhood issues. These issues can be found by checking local or neighborhood web pages or reading editorials in your local newspaper.

- Contributing to local newsletters with fire department related articles.

WEB PAGES

As more people use computers, so is their ability to get information distributed faster and easier. Web pages should be used by the fire department as a bulletin board. Web pages are an excellent and relatively easy way to post a message or an article for anyone to read.

Any information posted to a web page should be up to date and posted in a timely manner. Someone from the department should have the responsibility for updating the site frequently and on a regular basis. If it is not kept current, people will lose interest and stop checking it for information and updates.

Several items can be posted to a web page. These include the following:

- News releases

- Current issues

- Basic information about the department and services

- Fire and life safety tips

- Updates about purchases

- Departmental policies and procedures

- Information on how to contact departmental officials.

INTERGOVERNMENTAL RELATIONS

Counties, cities, districts, parish, boroughs, provincial, state, and federal governments all contribute to the local fire service. You should make every effort to recognize any contributions that they make to your department. This not only helps give your department a positive image, but you are also making governing agencies look good.

It is important that you do not isolate yourself or your department. Your department and other governmental jurisdictions should take advantage of each other's communication tools, such as interdepartmental and local newsletters, to reach a broader audience. You should make an effort to find out what is available in your area and then try to share resources with other governmental agencies.

MASS MEDIA ADVERTISEMENT

Consider Demographics

You need to consider the makeup of your audience, commonly called the *demographics*, when using the news media and advertisements. This allows you to create an advertisement that will be understood by the intended audience. For example, if the intended audience is a child, but the advertisement is written for an adult, the child will probably not be able to relate to the ad. (For more information on this, refer to **Appendix A**.) The citizens may not pay attention to advertisements or public service announcements if they do not feel the announcements relate to them. When preparing advertisements, try to make sure that the message is applicable towards the audience it is intended. Consider whether you need to create bilingual announcements.

Focus on Single Issue

You can use varied advertisements and announcements for a specific message. Focus on that issue so that the public is certain what you are trying to communicate to them. For example, if you are focusing on home safety, focus the ad on one point of home safety, such as smoke detectors, rather than having a number of issues in one advertisement. If a viewer is flooded with a number of topics, he or she will likely not remember the points of the message, but one clear and concise point will have a great impact.

Solicit Partnerships

Often, fire departments do not have the resources to create and maintain a great deal of community outreach. Other resources are available that can be used to fund a community outreach program. These include, but are not limited to:

- Local businesses
- Individuals
- The media
- School districts

Many of these organizations will donate items or provide financial resources to build a program. However, be careful that the department does not give the impression that they are endorsing a product or company, especially when dealing with life safety issues such as smoke detectors.

INTERNAL COMMUNICATIONS

With all the communication that goes on between the fire department and the public, you need to remember that your personnel need to be included in the information exchange. This allows them to be involved in the process and be more willing to participate in programs. The following lists recommended methods for distributing information internally:

- Post internal press releases

- Provide monthly newsletters

- Use technology such as TV stations, web sites, and e-mail

- Maintain an open-door policy

However, you may find other ways to provide information that is unique to your organization or personnel. Use whatever means works for you and your department. Regardless of how you choose to communicate with the department's personnel, remember that whatever you print or post will most likely become public knowledge. Do not print, post, or say anything that you do not want to be printed or said somewhere else later.

SUMMARY

Developing community relationships is essential for any fire department. No department can function without the needed support of the community it serves. As a result, the department must develop and maintain a strong working relationship with the community. As the public information officer, you have a pivotal role in developing and maintaining this relationship.

Appendix A
Readability Indexes

Reading ease is a major consideration in selecting written fire and life safety education materials. A seventh- to eighth-grade reading level is typical for adults in the United States. Daily newspapers are often written at about that reading level.

Follow simple guidelines when checking the readability of print materials:

- **Look for sentences written in the active voice**. Active sentences are shorter and easier to read than passive sentences. Examples of active and passive sentences follow:

  Active: Steve taught the audience how to test smoke detectors.

  Passive: The audience was taught how to test smoke detectors by Steve.

- **Look for short sentences with straightforward subject/verb construction**. Short sentences are easier to read than long sentences. Dependent clauses or phrases make reading more difficult. Examples follow:

Easy: The local smoke detector ordinance requires interconnected units. The ordinance took effect on January 1.

Difficult: The local smoke detector ordinance, which requires individual devices to be interconnected, became effective on January 1.

- **Look for a majority of one- and two-syllable words.** Generally, words of one or two syllables are easier to read (and comprehend) than words of three or more syllables.

Several indexes measure how easy (or difficult) a passage is to read. Commonly used indexes include a passive-sentence index (a simple percentage of passive sentences within a passage), the Flesch Reading Ease/Flesch Grade Level Index, and the Gunning FOG Index.

Flesch Index

The Flesch Index is based on a 100-word passage of the written material. This index counts the average number of words per sentence and the average number of syllables in the passage. Grade level and reading ease are matched to each other.

Gunning FOG Index

The Gunning FOG Index, on the other hand, combines the overall sentence length with the number of words containing more than one syllable per sentence.

To establish a FOG Index, perform the following steps:

Step 1: Select three 100-word passages from the material. Include the entire sentence that contains the 100th word.

Step 2: Calculate the average sentence length of one passage by dividing the number of words in the sample passage by the number of sentences.

Step 3: Count the number of words having three or more syllables. Do not include proper nouns (those that are capitalized), words that are a combination of short words (such as *chairperson* or *firefighter*), or words in which the third syllable is ed or es (such as *expanded*).

Step 4: Add together the average sentence length and the number of difficult words.

Step 5: Determine the average grade level of the passage by multiplying the sum of the average sentence length and the number of difficult words (computed in Step 4) by 0.4.

Step 6: Repeat Steps 2-5 for the remaining two passages.

Step 7: Find the average for all three passages by adding the grade levels for each passage and then dividing that answer by 3.

These indexes can be used manually or through some word processing programs. Whether the indexes are used manually or through the word processor, *the important point is to check whether sample materials are harder or easier to read than some standard that reflects the audience.* A highly precise test is not necessary as long as the fire and life safety educator knows whether written materials are "in the ballpark" for readability.

What happens when a 100-word passage from a fire and life safety brochure is examined according to readability indexes?

- Passive sentences — Only 1 sentence out of 11 was passive ("A smoke detector may be purchased..."). This yields an active sentence percentage of more than 90 percent.

- Flesch Reading Ease and Grade Level — The average sentence had 9 words (much lower or easier to read than the standard of 17). The 100-word passage contained 155 syllables, just slightly higher than the standard seventh- and eighth-grade level of 147. The tested passage would be rated between sixth-grade level (fairly easy) and eighth-grade level (standard).

- Gunning FOG Index — The average sentence had 9 words; the passage included 13 difficult words. T h e passage would be rated between eighth-grade level and ninth-grade level.